The Visual Guide to

Asperger's Syndrome: Meltdowns and Shutdowns

by Alis Rowe

Also by Alis Rowe

One Lonely Mind
978-0-9562693-0-0

The Girl with the Curly Hair - Asperger's and Me
978-0-9562693-2-4

The 1st Comic Book
978-0-9562693-1-7

The 2nd Comic Book
978-0-9562693-4-8

The 3rd Comic Book
978-0-9562693-3-1

The 4th Comic Book
978-15086839-7-1

The 5th Comic Book
978-15309879-3-1

Websites:
www.thegirlwiththecurlyhair.co.uk
www.thecurlyhairconsultancy.com
www.theliftingplace.com

Social Media:
www.facebook.com/thegirlwiththecurlyhair
www.twitter.com/curlyhairedalis

The Visual Guide to

Asperger's Syndrome: Meltdowns and Shutdowns

by Alis Rowe

Lonely Mind Books
London

For people on the autism spectrum and the people around them

hello

I'll be honest and say that I don't consider meltdowns and shutdowns to be my area of expertise (other than I experience them), nor are they amongst my favourite aspects of ASD to write about! They are however, very important to understand as they are a very common and debilitating part of living with autism.

In this book, I describe what meltdowns and shutdowns are, why they might occur, and some things autistic people can do to help themselves, and things loved ones can do to help them too.

I hope you find this book helpful!

Alis aka The Girl with the Curly Hair

Contents

OVERLOAD

It is thought that PEOPLE ON THE AUTISTIC SPECTRUM EXPERIENCE THE WORLD MORE INTENSELY, USING MORE MENTAL EFFORT THAN NEUROTYPICAL PEOPLE

This can cause a PERSON TO FEEL "OVERLOADED"

Meltdowns and shutdowns are typical responses to feeling overloaded

One way of thinking about overload is to consider that a PERSON ON THE AUTISTIC SPECTRUM has difficulty filtering out all the different sensory information (such as lights, sounds, smells and sights)

Whereas a NEUROTYPICAL PERSON can filter out any sensory information that's unimportant, irrelevant or unpleasant, an AUTISTIC PERSON might not be able to

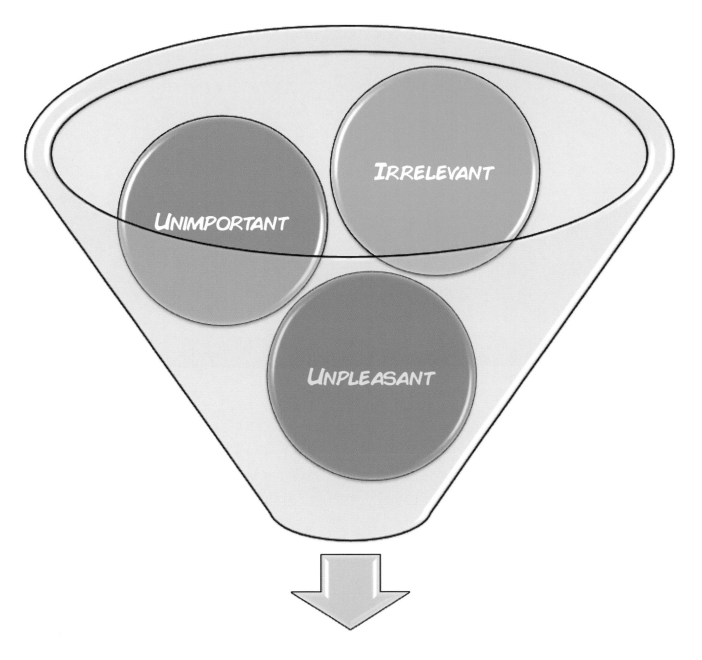

FOR EXAMPLE, WHEN THE GIRL WITH THE CURLY HAIR MEETS UP WITH HER FRIEND IN A CAFE FOR A CHAT, THEIR EXPERIENCES ARE SO DIFFERENT...

Many things become overloaded...

A CIRCUIT	BLOWS

A BOAT	SINKS

A BRIDGE	COLLAPSES

A TRAIN	WON'T STOP

A COMPUTER	WON'T START

AN AUTISTIC PERSON	MELTS OR SHUTS DOWN

EVERYBODY FEELS OVERLOADED AT TIMES

AUTISTIC PEOPLE HOWEVER, MIGHT EXPERIENCE THEIR SORT OF OVERLOAD A BIT DIFFERENTLY...

THEY MAY FEEL OVERLOADED BY THINGS THAT NEUROTYPICAL PEOPLE HARDLY NOTICE...

	Reality	Perceived

THEY MAY FEEL OVERLOADED MORE OFTEN...

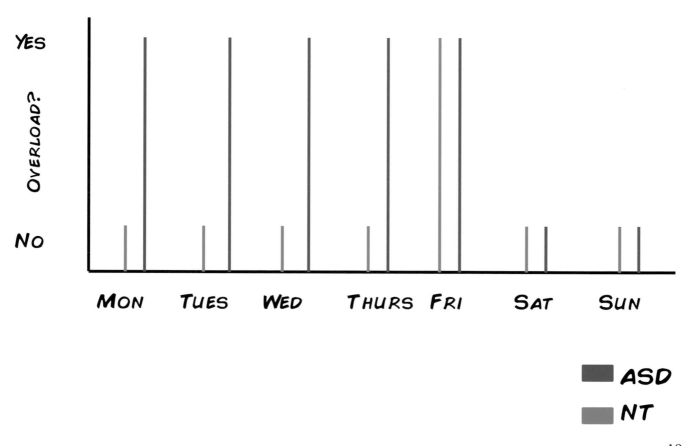

OR MORE STRONGLY...

OUR BRAINS ARE ALWAYS PROCESSING AND REGULATING THE SENSORY INFORMATION ('INPUT') FROM OUR ENVIRONMENT

AN AUTISTIC PERSON'S BRAIN MIGHT BE UNABLE TO PROCESS THIS INPUT PROPERLY

SO IT FEELS LIKE THERE IS "TOO MUCH INPUT!"

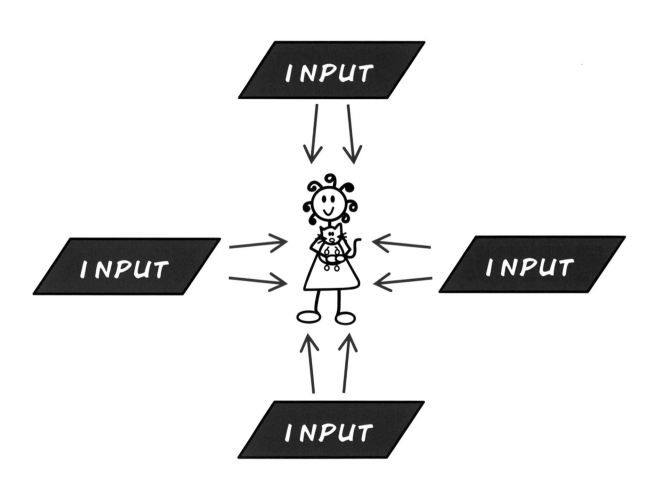

NEUROTYPICALS PROCESS THIS INPUT AUTOMATICALLY, WHEREAS FOR AUTISTIC PEOPLE, IT'S A MUCH MORE MANUAL EFFORT (AKIN TO THE EFFORT INVOLVED TAKING THE STAIRS VS AN ESCALATOR):

Escalator

Stairs

No wonder autistic people feel exhausted a lot of the time... exhausted in a public environment and exhausted by the time they get home!

WHAT IS 'INPUT'?

Input can be sensory information

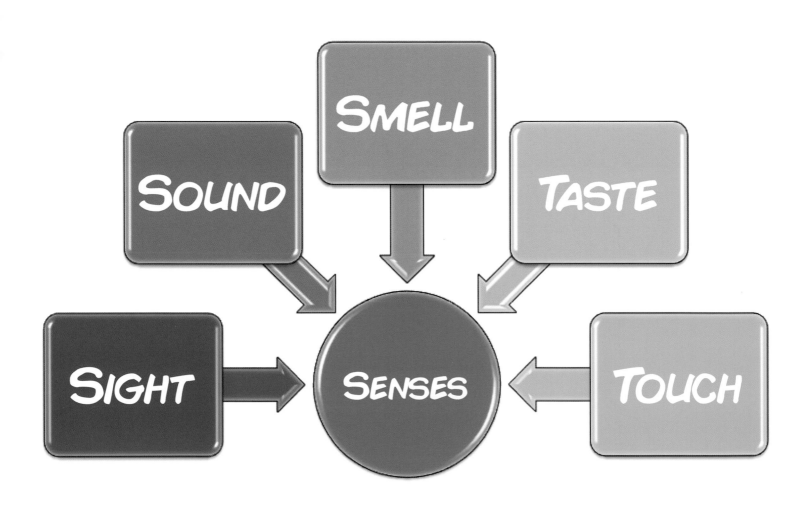

THE GIRL WITH THE CURLY HAIR HAS COME UP WITH STRATEGIES TO REDUCE THE AMOUNT OF SENSORY INPUT

IF THERE IS TOO MUCH NOISE...

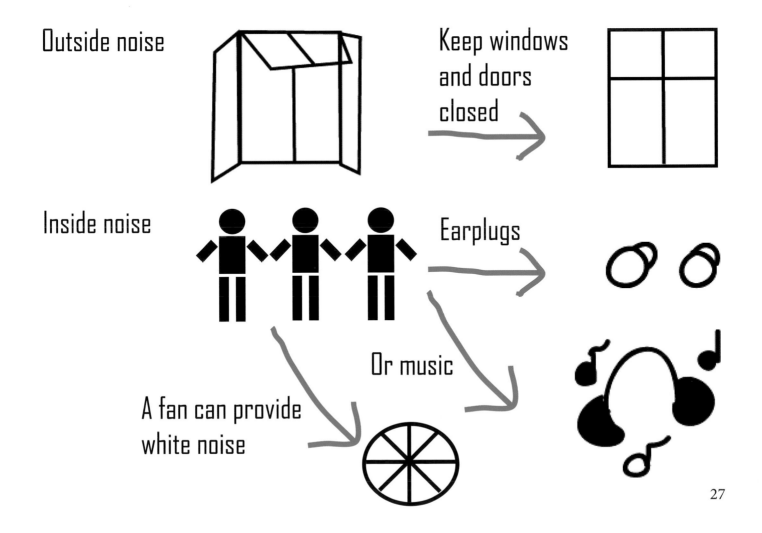

Outside noise

Keep windows and doors closed

Inside noise

Earplugs

Or music

A fan can provide white noise

IF THERE IS TOO MUCH LIGHT...

Sunlight coming through windows → Blackout blinds

Bright lighting → Tinted glasses

Open workspace → Closed workspace

IF THERE ARE UNPLEASANT OR OVERBEARING SMELLS...

Fragrance-free body wash and shampoo

Sniffing a bottle of lavendar oil can mask unpleasant smells

You can buy strong-smelling nasal creams

Her loved ones don't wear perfume

How The Girl with the Curly Hair copes with touch...

People approach from the front, never the back
And they always ask before they touch her

She finds and wears the fabric she is most comfortable with

Cotton
~~Polyester~~
~~Acrylic~~
~~Denim~~

And sleeps with a heavy duvet or a weighted blanket

She's fussy about how things taste too, and prefers to eat only a small variety of plain foods

She does however still try to be healthy, and makes sure she eats things from each of the food groups every day

She tries to keep eating foods high in fat and sugar to a minimum

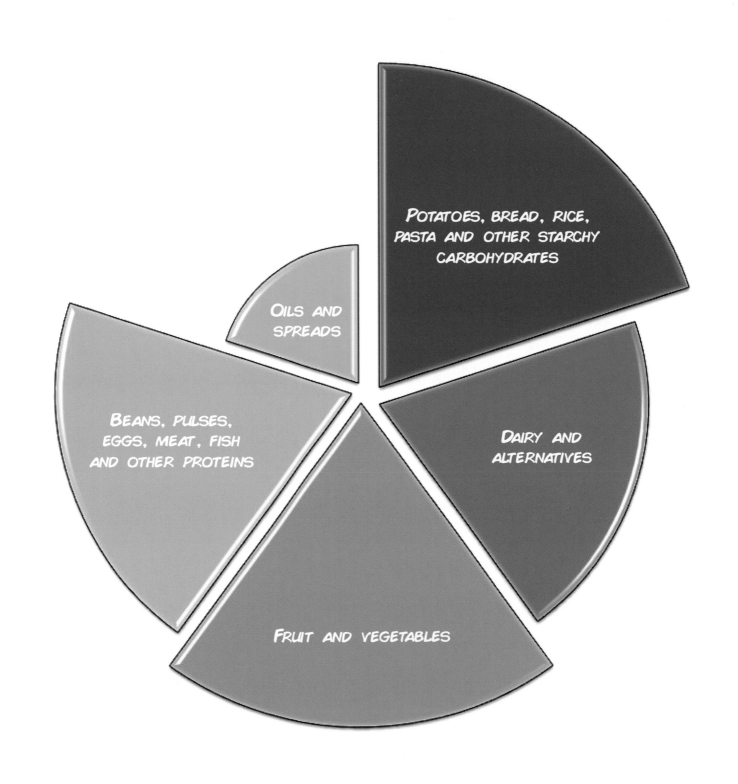

SHE MIGHT PREFER TO KEEP FOODS
SEPARATE AND NOT TOUCHING:

SOMETIMES IT'S THE TEXTURE THAT PUTS
HER OFF EATING SOMETHING. TEXTURE
CAN USUALLY BE CHANGED THOUGH, FOR
EXAMPLE, CARROTS:

INPUT CAN ALSO BE TO DO WITH SOCIALISING (SOCIAL INFORMATION)

AUTISTIC PEOPLE HAVE DIFFICULTIES WITH SOCIAL INTERACTION AND SOCIAL COMMUNICATION

THIS MEANS THAT THEY DON'T PROCESS AND UNDERSTAND 'SOCIAL INFORMATION' (BODY LANGUAGE, WORDS, TONE OF VOICE) AS AUTOMATICALLY AS NEUROTYPICAL PEOPLE AND SO SOCIAL INTERACTIONS ARE HARD WORK!

AUTISTIC PEOPLE HAVE A DYAD OF IMPAIRMENTS*

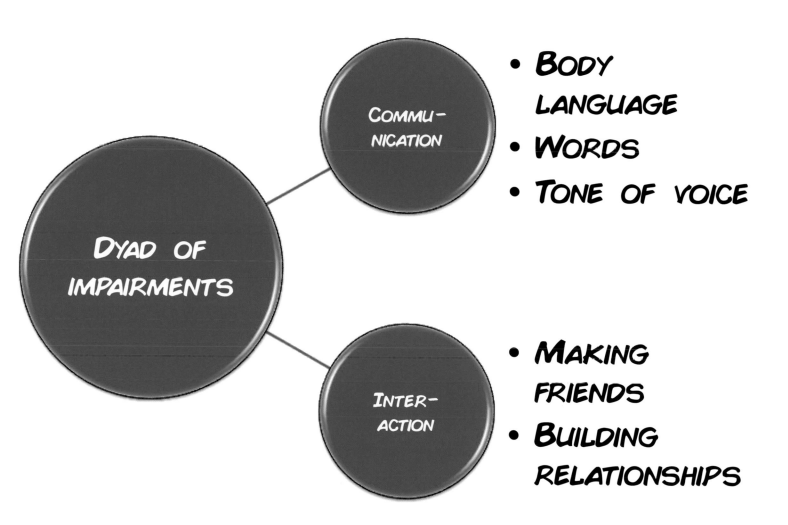

COMMU-NICATION
- BODY LANGUAGE
- WORDS
- TONE OF VOICE

DYAD OF IMPAIRMENTS

INTER-ACTION
- MAKING FRIENDS
- BUILDING RELATIONSHIPS

* American Psychiatric Association. (2013). Diagnostic and statistical manual of mental disorders (5th ed.). Arlington, VA: American Psychiatric Publishing

SOCIAL CHALLENGES CAUSE THE GIRL WITH THE CURLY HAIR TO FEEL LIKE SHE'S LIVING ON THE "WRONG PLANET". EITHER SHE VIEWS HERSELF AS AN ALIEN...

Mirror

...OR SHE VIEWS EVERYBODY ELSE AS ALIENS:

Glass pane

Socialising and relating to others is difficult

She has to put in an enormous amount of effort any time she interacts with someone

Interactions can therefore contribute to 'overload' too

BECAUSE OF THEIR DYAD OF IMPAIRMENTS, THE GIRL WITH THE CURLY HAIR THINKS THAT AUTISTIC PEOPLE HAVE LESS CAPACITY FOR SOCIAL INTERACTION THAN NEUROTYPICAL PEOPLE

THIS MEANS THAT, WHEN SOCIALISING, THEY MIGHT FEEL TIRED OR OVERWHELMED SOONER OR EASIER THAN OTHER PEOPLE

THIS IS KNOWN AS 'SOCIAL ENERGY THEORY'

EXTROVERTS GAIN SOCIAL ENERGY FROM SOCIAL INTERACTION – BUT WHEN THEIR TANK IS FULL IS WHEN THEY'VE HAD ENOUGH. AN ASD EXTROVERT TANK IS SMALLER THAN AN NT EXTROVERT TANK

INTROVERTS LOSE SOCIAL ENERGY FROM SOCIAL INTERACTION AND WHEN THEY THEIR TANK IS EMPTY THEY'VE HAD ENOUGH. AN ASD INTROVERT TANK IS SMALLER THAN AN NT INTROVERT TANK

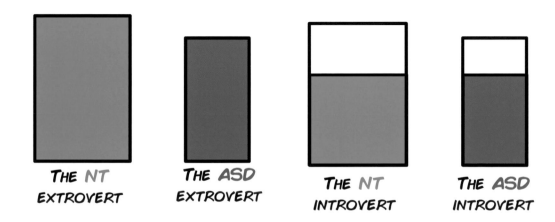

THE NT EXTROVERT

THE ASD EXTROVERT

THE NT INTROVERT

THE ASD INTROVERT

TOO MUCH SOCIAL INTERACTION THEREFORE, CAN ALSO LEAD TO OVERLOAD

IT'S HUGELY IMPORTANT FOR AUTISTIC PEOPLE TO HAVE PLENTY OF ALONE OR DOWN TIME TO REGENERATE THEIR SOCIAL ENERGY

How does The Girl with the Curly Hair reduce the likelihood of social overload?

She avoids going out at peak times. For example, she goes to the supermarket during the week rather than at the weekends

She prefers to talk to people one to one, in a quiet environment

Loved ones are respectful of the way she views the world. It is different, not wrong

She wears tinted glasses and earplugs a lot, or she might listen to music. She keeps her hood up

She asks friends not to put pressure on her to attend their social events. After she has said "no" once, she does not want to be asked multiple times

She asks friends to let her know in advance if they need to change or cancel their plans

She asks friends to try extra hard to be on time when meeting her

Her loved ones know to allow her to spend time doing things she enjoys and encourage it

She asks friends to say what they mean and mean what they say

Struggling to process all this sensory and social input can lead to an AUTISTIC PERSON feeling overloaded and likely to have either a meltdown or a shutdown

MELTDOWNS

How does The Girl with the Curly Hair describe meltdowns?

I CURL UP IN A BALL OR FLOP ON TO THE FLOOR

I USUALLY SHOUT, SCREAM AND CRY

IN WORST CASE SCENARIOS, I MIGHT TRY TO HIT AND KICK PEOPLE OR THINGS

I MIGHT PULL OUT MY HAIR OR BANG MY HEAD AGAINST THE WALL

I MIGHT BREAK THINGS

I FLAP MY HANDS WILDLY

I MIGHT RUN AROUND SHOUTING "NO, NO, NO!"

AS I GET OLDER, MY PHYSICAL OUTBURSTS ARE LESS COMMON BUT EMOTIONAL OUTBURSTS STILL OCCUR

THE GIRL WITH THE CURLY HAIR HIGHLIGHTS SOME SIGNS OF IMPENDING MELTDOWN AND SUGGESTS WAYS TO AVOID IT:

LOOK AT THE BIG PICTURE

- ARE THEY TIRED, FRUSTRATED, STRESSED OR HYPERACTIVE? ARE THEY UNWELL OR IN PAIN?
- ARE THEY DOING SOMETHING THAT IS OUT OF THEIR NORMAL ROUTINE?
- WHAT IS THE CURRENT SENSORY EXPOSURE LIKE?

RECOGNISE THE PHYSICAL SIGNS

- ARE THEY SQUEEZING THEIR PEN TOO TIGHTLY?
- ARE THEY MAKING MORE NOISE THAN USUAL?
- ARE THEY FLAPPING, ROCKING OR FIDGETING?
- ARE THEY MORE WITHDRAWN THAN USUAL?
- DO THEY LOOK PHYSICALLY UNCOMFORTABLE?

DECREASE THE LIKELIHOOD OF MELTDOWN

- TAKE THEM AWAY FROM THE TRIGGER OR TAKE THE TRIGGER AWAY FROM THEM
- SPEAK TO THEM IN A CALM, SOOTHING VOICE
- RUB THEIR BACK/HOLD THEM (IF THEY LIKE THAT – SOME PEOPLE GET A LOT OF COMFORT FROM FIRM TOUCH, OTHERS HATE IT), PROVIDE A SAFETY ANCHOR
- MAKE AN EXCUSE FOR THEM

WHEN I'M ABOUT TO HAVE A MELTDOWN, THERE IS A TINY PART OF MY MIND THAT SAYS, VERY LOGICALLY, "STOP RIGHT NOW" AND "YOU HAVE A CHOICE NOW ABOUT WHAT IS GOING TO HAPPEN NEXT"...
...BUT ANOTHER, MUCH BIGGER, PART OF MY MIND EITHER IGNORES THIS OR EVEN SORT OF RETALIATES BACK AND SAYS "I DON'T CARE!" AND THEN THE MELTDOWN JUST HAPPENS

Meltdowns may seem the same as tantrums but there are some significant differences:

Tantrum vs Meltdown
By The Girl with the Curly Hair

Tantrum	Both	Meltdown
* Driven by a want or goal * Usually it's because they want something * They check you're paying attention to their behaviour * They act this way in front of an audience * Once they've got what they want, the behaviour will cease	Screaming Kicking Shouting Stomping Swearing Biting etc.	* Driven by a reaction to something * A reaction to overload or feeling overwhelmed * They don't care if they get attention or not * Their behaviour will continue even without an audience * There is no goal. The behaviour will only cease once they've calmed down or when a loved one has helped them regain control

The Girl with the Curly Hair says the simplest way to differentiate between a tantrum and a meltdown is to observe whether the "aim" is to get attention (and once they get what they want, the tantrum will stop)

WHEN A MELTDOWN IS HAPPENING, HERE ARE SOME THINGS A LOVED ONE CAN DO TO HELP:

MAKE SURE <u>THEY</u> ARE SAFE

- IF YOU ARE OUT, GET THEM HOME OR TAKE THEM SOMEWHERE PRIVATE AND QUIET
- DO NOT LET THEM WANDER OFF IN CASE THEY HURT THEMSELVES (REMEMBER, THEY ARE MOST LIKELY OUT OF CONTROL AT THIS TIME)
- SOME PEOPLE LIKE TO BE HELD VERY TIGHTLY, OTHERS MAY HATE IT
- IS THERE A PARTICULAR COMFORT ITEM YOU CAN GIVE THEM?
- CAN YOU GIVE THEM AN ALTERNATIVE FOR SELF-HARMING, E.G. PAPER TO RIP UP, A PILLOW TO HIT, ICE CUBES TO THROW IN THE BATH?

MAKE SURE THEIR <u>ENVIRONMENT</u> IS SAFE

- MAKE SURE THERE ARE NO POTENTIALLY DANGEROUS OBJECTS LYING AROUND
- CLEAR AWAY TOYS THEY MIGHT TRIP OVER, REMOVE GLASS THEY COULD CUT THEMSELVES ON, ETC.

IT'S NOT A GOOD IDEA TO ATTEMPT TO ASK THE PERSON "WHAT'S WRONG?" OR TO ASK "HOW CAN I HELP?" DURING A MELTDOWN

THIS IS THE NATURAL THING FOR MANY NEUROTYPICALS TO WANT TO DO

BUT TRYING TO COMMUNICATE WITH SOMEONE WHILST THEY ARE HAVING A MELTDOWN IS JUST CREATING EVEN MORE INPUT!

IT'S BEST TO TALK ABOUT THE MELTDOWN AFTER IT HAS HAPPENED

49

AN AUTISTIC PERSON THEMSELVES COULD TRY TO RECOGNISE THEIR OWN SIGNS AND SYMPTOMS SO THAT THEY KNOW WHEN THEY'RE BEGINNING TO FEEL OVERLOADED, E.G.

SIGNS	SYMPTOMS (FEELINGS)
• TALKING A LOT • NOT TALKING • SWEATING • PACING • FIDGETING • FLAPPING	• BUTTERFLIES • EARS FEEL HOT • SICK • IRRITABLE

THEN THEY COULD LEARN WHAT TO DO WHEN THEY FEEL THIS WAY, BEFORE A MELTDOWN HAPPENS

CALMING STRATEGIES OR LEAVING THE SITUATION QUICKLY ENOUGH COULD ACTUALLY PREVENT THE MELTDOWN FROM OCCURRING

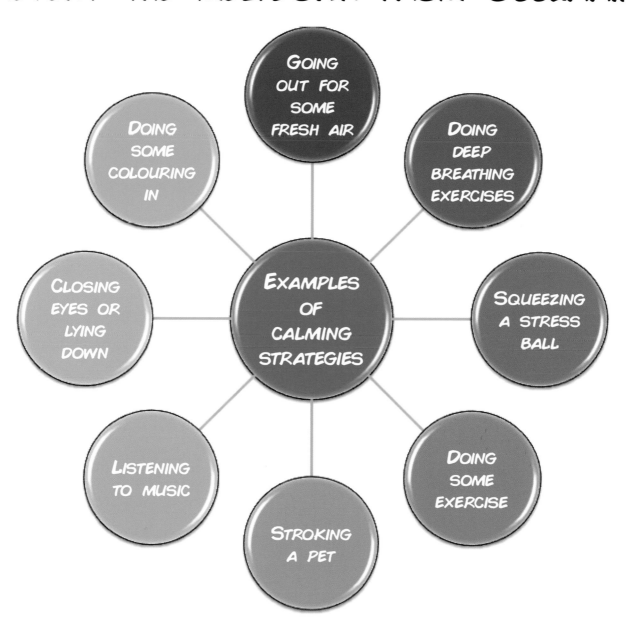

ALWAYS MAKE SURE THE PERSON HAS AN EXIT STRATEGY...

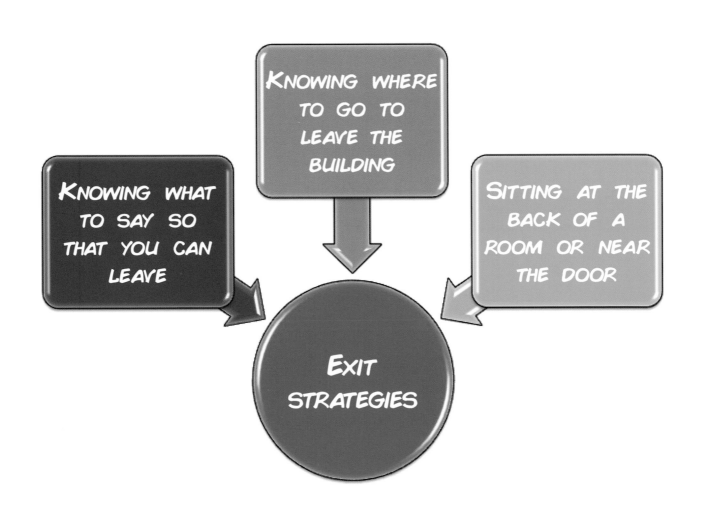

A PERSON MAY HAVE SOME UNCOMFORTABLE FEELINGS AFTER THEIR MELTDOWN

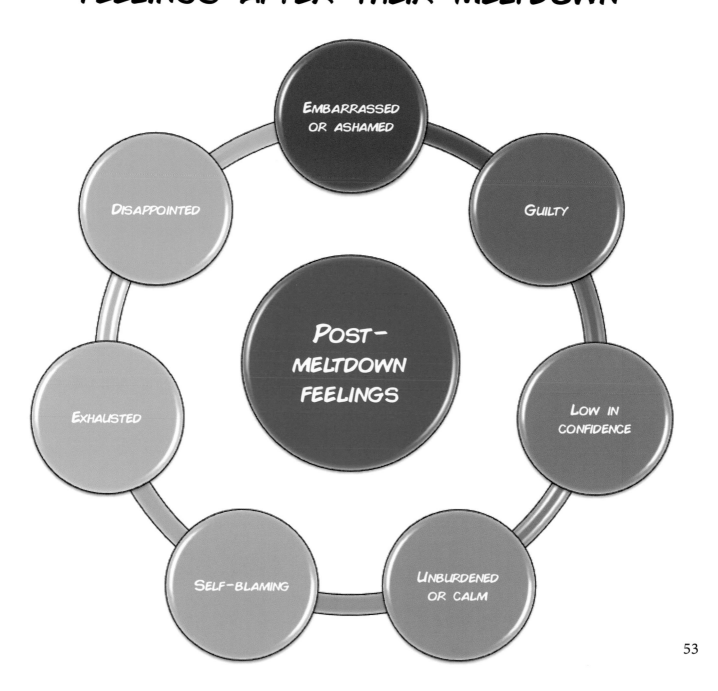

HERE ARE SOME THINGS PEOPLE CAN DO TO HELP THEMSELVES AND SOME SUGGESTIONS ON HOW OTHERS CAN HELP AN AUTISTIC LOVED ONE AFTER A MELTDOWN

HOW THE AUTISTIC PERSON CAN HELP THEMSELVES

- CLEAR YOUR DIARY
- REMOVE WORD 'SHOULD' FROM YOUR VOCABULARY
- RAISE AWARENESS OF ASD AND MELTDOWNS IN THE COMMUNITY
- IF IT HAPPENED IN A PUBLIC PLACE, CONSIDER WRITING A SHORT, EXPLANATORY NOTE
- IN THE LONG RUN, RECOGNISING AND MINIMISING YOUR TRIGGERS IS GOING TO BE THE BEST, MOST MAINTAINABLE SOLUTION

OTHERS CAN HELP TOO

- REASSURE THAT YOU STILL SEE THEM AS THE SAME PERSON
- LEARN ABOUT MELTDOWNS AND UNDERSTAND THAT THEY ARE OFTEN OUT OF THE PERSON'S CONTROL
- TRULY LISTEN IF THEY WANT TO TELL YOU WHY IT HAPPENED
- REMAIN ENCOURAGING: "I KNOW YOU ARE VERY UPSET RIGHT NOW BUT I ALSO KNOW THAT YOU ARE VERY GOOD AT CALMING YOURSELF DOWN"
- BE A TEAM AND BE GOAL-FOCUSED: "WE HAVE A PROBLEM BUT WE ARE GOING TO FIX IT"
- CLEAR THEIR DIARY OR REARRANGE THEIR UPCOMING PLANS

SHUTDOWNS

SHUTDOWNS ARE ANOTHER COMMON WAY OF RESPONDING TO OVERLOAD

HOW DOES THE GIRL WITH THE CURLY HAIR DESCRIBE SHUTDOWNS?

I MIGHT JUST SIT SILENTLY AND ROCK

I FEEL VERY TIRED AND WANT TO SLEEP

I STARE INTO SPACE AND, TO OTHERS, I HAVE A VERY BLANK FACIAL EXPRESSION

MY BODY IS PRESENT BUT MY MIND IS NOT

I CAN'T REALLY SPEAK. THE WORDS WON'T COME OUT

I WITHDRAW FOR A DAY OR TWO, SOMETIMES MORE. I JUST NEED TO BE ON MY OWN

I WANT TO BE IN THE DARK. IF POSSIBLE, I'LL GET UNDER THE COVERS, UNDER A TABLE OR INSIDE A CUPBOARD

I FEEL "BLACKED OUT," "REMOVED" AND NUMB

I'M AWARE I EXIST BUT I'M UNABLE TO CONNECT WITH EXISTENCE

It might be helpful to think of shutdowns as a sort of 'protection mechanism' – shutting off the brain so that it can't receive any more input

They might be a way of regenerating more social energy and a way to calm down after having had too much sensory input too

When someone is recovering from a shutdown, the focus should be conserving energy and making things as easy to do as possible

HERE ARE SOME THINGS PEOPLE CAN DO TO HELP THEMSELVES AND SOME SUGGESTIONS ON HOW OTHERS CAN HELP AN AUTISTIC LOVED ONE DURING AND AFTER A SHUTDOWN

HOW TO HELP SOMEONE COMMUNICATE

- REDUCE EYE CONTACT
- KEEP LANGUAGE SHORT AND CONCISE
- ASK QUESTIONS THAT ONLY REQUIRE VERY BRIEF OR ONE-WORD ANSWERS
- WRITE/TEXT/DRAW INSTEAD

HOW THEY COULD HELP THEMSELVES

- FIND ALTERNATIVE WAYS TO COMMUNICATE SUCH AS THROUGH WRITING/TEXTING AND DRAWING

HOW TO HELP SOMEONE EAT

- MAKE AND BRING TO THEM THEIR FAVOURITE OR 'NORMAL' FOOD
- STICK TO THEIR REGULAR EATING TIME
- CONSIDER 'EASIER' TEXTURES FOR THEM TO EAT, SUCH AS LIQUIDS OR SOFT FOODS

HOW THEY COULD HELP THEMSELVES

- PREPARE FOR SHUTDOWNS IN ADVANCE AND HAVE MEALS READY AND AVAILABLE IN THE FRIDGE OR IN THE FREEZER

How to help someone with personal hygiene

- Run their bath for them
- Put out bath mat, towel, etc.
- Have their clothes ready for them when they come out
- Wash or comb their hair
- Get their toothbrush and mouthwash ready

How they could help themselves

- Find alternative ways to maintain hygiene that use less energy, e.g. dry shampoo, keeping hair short as standard so it's easier to manage in the long term

How to help someone participate in hobbies

- Adapt their hobby so that it can be done at home or from their bedroom
- Talk to them about their hobby
- Try participating in their hobby alongside them

How they could help themselves

- Find alternative ways to pursue hobby, e.g. may not be able to go out but could do it at home or read about it instead, etc.

THE BEST WAY TO HELP YOUR ASD LOVED ONE IS TO TALK TO THEM ABOUT THEIR MELTDOWNS AND SHUTDOWNS WHEN THEY ARE IN THEIR 'NORMAL' STATE...

THE ASD PERSON THEMSELVES COULD LEARN TO KEEP TRACK OF WHAT THEY THINK CAUSED THE MELTDOWN OR SHUTDOWN, AND WORK OUT WAYS TO PREVENT IT FROM HAPPENING AGAIN

Many thanks for reading

Other books in The Visual Guides series at the time of writing:

Asperger's Syndrome
Asperger's Syndrome in 5-8 Year Olds
Asperger's Syndrome in 8-11 Year Olds
Asperger's Syndrome in 13-16 Year Olds
Asperger's Syndrome in 16-18 Year Olds
Asperger's Syndrome for the Neurotypical Partner
Asperger's Syndrome: Social Energy
Asperger's Syndrome and Anxiety
Asperger's Syndrome: Helping Siblings
Asperger's Syndrome and Puberty
Asperger's Syndrome: Meltdowns and Shutdowns (2)
Adapting Health Therapies for People on the Autism Spectrum
Asperger's Syndrome and Emotions
Asperger's Syndrome and Communication

New titles are continually being produced so keep an eye out!